HOW TO GROW THROUGH PTSD

A GUIDE FOR PERSONAL GROWTH THROUGH STRESS

Timothy R. Carter

ISBN: 9781652894506

You can get this book on audio. It can be found on
Audible, iTunes, and Amazon.com

Table of Contents

Chapter 1: How to Grow Through PTSD 1

Chapter 2: Whitewater Rapids 5

Chapter 3: When Loss Hits You Like Violent Rapids... 9

Chapter 4: Dam 11

   The Transitioning & Transformation Caused by
Change 12

Chapter 5: Disappointments Don't Have to Delete Our
Dreams 15

Chapter 6: Believe 19

Chapter 7: Post-Traumatic Growth 21

Chapter 8: Psychological Effects of Disappointments:
Trauma-Research on Post-Traumatic Growth 25

Chapter 9: The Post-Traumatic Growth Inventory 29

Chapter 10: Steps to Achieve Post-Traumatic Growth 33

Chapter 11: Begin the Process of Post-Traumatic
Growth 37

   Step 1: Shattered into a Million Pieces 37

Step 2: Getting Up & Building on Our Positives ..44

Step 3: From Broken to Better (Phoenix from the ashes)..51

Chapter 12: Another Way to Look at Things 55

Conclusion...59

References 61

About the Author 63

Other Books by 65

Timothy R. Carter 65

Connect with 66

Timothy R. Carter 66

Chapter 1

How to Grow Through PTSD

THIS BOOK IS a brief explanation of How to Grow Through PTSD. PTSD is also known as Post-Traumatic Stress Disorder.

How do we overcome a traumatic experience? To have emotional growth through trauma, we must:

- ☐ Start where we are, at rock bottom

- ☐ Build on the positive

- ☐ Help other people

Change can be one of the most difficult or one of the most joyous things we can experience in life. The inevitability of change is both frightening and exciting. Change has profound psychological effects. So, the title of this read should be rather long,

"How to Overcome Hard Times: Psychological Effects of Disappointments, Due to Trauma."

Many of us are comfortable within the realms of sameness and structure because predictability does not rattle us, scare us, or challenge us. Predictability involves the limited expenditure of any extra effort, kind of like floating on calm, cold water that gently goes around in circles or leads to a secure pond surrounded by trees. We can just lay back relax, dip our fingertips in the cold water, knowing that there is no risk of reaching an eventual, steep precipice.

We all learn, sooner or later, that there is no such thing as flowing through life, laid back, with our eyes closed. Eventually, the change will come and pry our eyes open, no matter how hard we try to keep them shut.

Difficult times help us (or forces us if we are exceptionally resistant) to progress. Because if left to our decision-making, we might choose to stay on the same, serene, and safe path where we do not see, feel, or encounter anything new. Few of us would voluntarily choose the course that shakes, pushes, and tips us over, nearly drowning us.

Hard times come in many different forms and sometimes come crashing down on us in the way of trauma or loss, failure, or disappointment. Throughout this book, I will be using the words 'trauma' and 'loss' interchangeably. It's similar to riding the river. Sometimes there are troubled waters. When change comes to us in these ways, we often find ourselves having to start from scratch. As if everything we have worked towards, invested in, or achieved is gone. We are left empty-handed, lost, alone, and broken.

Chapter 2

Whitewater Rapids

I WENT TO college and graduate school in Cleveland, Tennessee. We were close to the Ocoee River, which has world renown whitewater rapids. It was not uncommon to hear whitewater rapids lingo around campus because the students would go by the busloads to ride the wild water every day of the week.

We could use several different flotation devices, an inflatable tube, Kayak, a wave-punching paddle raft, an inflatable raft, and the list goes on.

Each device holds its pros and cons. For this book, we will be using a mixture of terms.

Ocoee River is (a small section of the Toccoa River), a 93-mile-long river that flows northwestward through the southern Appalachian

Mountains of the southeastern United States. The rapids here can become so severe that the Ocoee River held the 1996 Olympic whitewater canoe and kayak competition (NOC Ocoee River).

This read will utilize the adventure of whitewater rapids as a metaphor for life; it uses the water flow as a symbol of difficult situations.

- ☐ **Class I:** gentle moving water

- ☐ **Class II:** water moving slightly faster than gentle. It's running just enough to splash over

- ☐ The side of the flotation device

- ☐ **Class III:** is starting to pick up momentum. At this speed, the splash is big enough to

- ☐ soak us head to foot

- ☐ **Class IV:** the water is taking on a strong personally now. The big splashes will scare us

- ☐ as we try to paddle through the intense whitewater

- **Class V:** is where the violent rapids are enough to give nightmares. The intensity of

- violence will get our heart pumping much faster than average. Class V is the highest level

- of energy anyone can navigate safely and have an expectation of safety

- **Class VI** is the forbidden whitewater; the brutality is so intense people die. Note, the Ocoee River don't have Class VI.

We should have the luxury to love every minute of life. However, our lives become difficult from time to time. We are at the mercy of the river of life! The water flow can change dramatically and suddenly. This shift in water change is what creates stress. The intensity of the pressure directly correlates to the class of troubled water and how well we can navigate throughout the season of rapids.

Chapter 3

When Loss Hits You Like Violent Rapids

TRAUMA AND LOSS mean different things to different people. An event that can shock and create profound effects on one person can be laughed off and considered benign by another person. Stressful experiences and stressors affect us depending on various factors, individual differences such as past experiences, the level of maturity, culture, and personality type. The event or occurrence itself can differ from person to person, but the stages of change whereby we all cope with and process loss are surprisingly very similar. We might take different paths, be given different events, and encounter various obstacles, but we're all on the same journey down the river of life.

Each of us will respond to the river of life in our way during each stage of classification. We will do whatever it takes not to drown.

When we went to the Ocoee River to ride the whitewater rapids, our River Rat (river guide) told us, "Don't fight the rapids, relax, and go with the flow." When we try to fight the water, our flotation device is capsized and battered upon the rocks. During hard times, our natural response is to fight against the stressor. The more we resist, the more difficulty we cause ourselves. Just as the wild water will beat us against the obstacles in the river, stress has a powerful way of beating us against a blending of challenges.

Chapter 4

Dam

THE DAM MODERATES the release of water. The dam symbolizes the control panel of life. These are things providing stability and reasonable regulation such as job, family, health, and anything else where we find that sense of security and safety.

The adjustments to the dam will alter things in the river of life, such as:

☐ The cliffs of the river

☐ Depth of water

☐ Speed of the water

Modifications to the dam will create stress to some degree. This stress usually becomes traumatic, impacting us in emotional, cognitive, and physical ways, taking a severe toll on our mind and body. Some people experience crippling sadness, worry, fear, or panic. These symptoms can take on the physical form of headaches, stomach pain, loss of energy, insomnia, among many other painful physical symptoms.

These feelings and experiences occur when transformation happens faster than we can process. We feel unable to handle the stress. We feel cheated, scared, confused, and punished. We feel like, "Why me… why this… why now?" We wish to turn back time so that things can go back to the way they were before, back to normal. We want the predictability and sameness that we once had before these waters became troubled. The rapids have come and turned our life upside down, presumably robbing us of our dreams, goals, illusions, and happiness.

The Transitioning & Transformation Caused by Change

When the dam is adjusted, our comfortable Class I river of life can suddenly shift to Class IV or even higher. This sudden shift creates a feeling of panic.

Just as with a natural river, the river of life contains many patches of rapids. A section of calm water separates each parcel of troubled water.

After the trauma, there is a season of

☐ Mourning

☐ Wanting to give up

☐ Giving up

☐ Then a period of "What do I do now?

14

Chapter 5

Disappointments Don't Have to Delete Our Dreams

THERE IS A phenomenon known as Post-Traumatic Growth (PTG), which occurs when a person makes a positive change as a result of a vital negative (or actual) life event. PTG (the opposite of Post-Traumatic Stress) occurs when an individual undergoes emotional growth as a result of an impacting event and becomes inspired by this experience, deriving a renewed meaning and purpose in life (Hefferon, K., Grealy, M., & Mutrie, N. (2009).

The Thriver Model explains it's the way we process and perceive the activity that contributes to interpersonal growth (Mangelsdorf & Eid, 2015). Although it takes time, and a period of mourning to be able to see change as something positive. It's how we perceive and act on the difference that will determine the great places we will go from this point forward.

When the water calms, we can find ourselves in a Pool-Drop River for a while. Pool-Drop River is a small pool of calm water after a section of rapids, which is excellent for catching our breath to regroup our thoughts and relax in our inflatable raft.

Despite any setback with trauma, we can persevere and reach our goals and dreams. Each small goal will serve as fuel need to catapult us to the direct path towards our vision. We can achieve our goals not only despite change but also because of progression. The calm waters don't require action; therefore, they don't lead to high achievement. This tranquil path teaches nothing and will not help to build the strength and character that we need to confront the challenges that accompany great performances.

This difficult time will expose the inter resilience that we never knew existed.

We must develop depth and character to navigate the rapids. The rocky waters are what builds muscle and show us how we can overcome anything. This difficult time will expose the inter resilience that we never knew existed.

Think of the most prominent role model or the most significant and influential figures of the present day. Think of the most influential persons throughout history. None of these individuals had a straight and comfortable path that led them to achieve great things. It is no coincidence that these individuals describe the unpredictable rapid they had to navigate before they made a positive difference in the world.

Most of us have experienced the darkness that occurs after a life-altering loss. We have fallen, we have lost hope. We have felt abandoned and forgotten. Each one of us has felt like we have no options. Our broken heart and soul are an entryway to a life full of experiences, achievements, happiness, and real, genuine self-fulfillment.

Chapter 6

Believe

BELIEVE:

- ☐ This transformation is our unique purpose

- ☐ Our ability is enough to accept this experience

- ☐ It's time to move forward through our journey

- ☐ We will develop the courage and strength within each of us

We can inspire others to see life changes as opportunities to grow and interpersonal development. (My journey is not shared here). Often, we lose ourselves to find who we are. We can become genuinely lost in the depths of personal tragedy, but we can discover a resilient side of self that we never knew existed. It's possible to develop the skills to understand *How to Overcome Hard Times. Life is sweeter after the uncertain waters. Our adventure is better because of the strength we gain through the troubled waters.*

One day we will look back at these difficult years of life and smile in amazement, as we connect the dots and realize that what was lost was a life-changing gift. The trauma was a chance to achieve some of the most amazing things in life. The journey is continuous, and we're still learning and growing through this process.

Chapter 7

Post-Traumatic Growth

POSITIVE CHANGE, PERSONAL growth, and development of the self are experiences described by individuals who undergo PTG. PTG is not a new concept; instead, it has gained a more significant universality in recent decades. This popularity is because researchers have investigated how adverse life events cause PTSD. Experts have also studied the life-altering, positive growth as a result of traumatic events.

Not only is PTG not a novel concept, but every day people have also used various terms to describe the experiences typical of PTG. Think of all the times you have heard the sayings:

☐ Make lemons out of lemonade

☐ Turn negatives into positives

☐ No pain, no gain

☐ What doesn't kill you makes you stronger

These seem to be cliché, but they are essential and real ways that people have been describing PTG for generations.

The desire to not only adapt to a negative situation but also persevere and attribute the experience of the trauma and difficulty of life to a higher and more meaningful purpose is not only a healthy way of coping but is an effective way of getting through hard times.

We cannot always anticipate when the dam will be adjusted. We're not in control of the things that impact our lives. We all, to varying degrees, like control.

Taking this concept of control, a step further; By having a positive attitude. This concept is also about deriving meaning from what happens to us. As we learn from this, it helps us to become stronger. We are emitting the ultimate control over adverse/traumatic events.

Experiencing PTG is similar to looking life and destiny in the face (if these concepts were to be personified) saying, "*Ha! You don't control me. I control you.*"

Chapter 8

Psychological Effects of Disappointments: Trauma-Research on Post-Traumatic Growth

MANY RESEARCHERS, SCHOLARS, and authors have investigated, measured, and discussed the concept of PTG. Trauma can cause changes in the deep-rooted beliefs that people have ascribed to their whole life. Trauma will initiate the process of acquiring an improved and more genuine value and belief system (Sheikh, 2008).

People who experience PTG can also develop the ability to manage any future emotional distress better. The PTG that we acquire as a result of trauma can improve us forever so that we face any future loss with greater inner strength and ability to cope (Sheikh, 2008). In other words, when the waters of life become troubled with something difficult, we go through a sort of *rite of passage*. We struggle, we want to give up, but we keep going anyway. We get through the difficulty. This process causes something to click deep within. Maybe this level is:

- ☐ An emotional level

- ☐ The neurological level

- ☐ Feasibly both

When we realize whatever we realize we are different from that moment forward. We are reborn into a different level of awareness and meaning. We have thicker skin to protect us from anything else that life might throw our way. The spark of resilience is burning within brighter than ever.

The researchers Tedeschi and Calhoun (1996), developed a PTG Inventory, which is a test that measures the positive outcomes that have resulted from a person's traumatic experiences.

The inventory assesses several categories that the authors believe are related to PTG. If the test taker scores above a certain score threshold in these areas, they are said to have experienced positive outcomes from their traumatic or painful life experience. The different categories include: *New Possibilities, Relating to Others, Personal Strength, Spiritual Change, and Appreciation of Life*. The authors tested the inventory on research participants to see how well the list measured these PTG traits (Tedeschi & Calhoun, 1996).

28

Chapter 9

The Post-Traumatic Growth Inventory

PSYCHOLOGISTS ARE ENCOURAGED to evaluate the achievement of growth within five areas (Tedeschi & Calhoun, 1996):

1. Appreciation of life- One doesn't have to show growth in all five regions equally. Everyone grows within each category at their own pace. The client who has achievement in growth shows a marked improvement in his/her outlook on life in general.

2. Relationships with others-As a result of personal growth, one should have a measurable improvement in one's relationships; family, co-workers, employer,

employees, children, spouse, church, and community.

3. New possibilities in life- As a result of PTG, he/she should show a piece of remarkable evidence that he/she can see a brighter future.

4. Personal strength- PTG can be recognized by emotional and mental strength in the one who has grown through trauma.

5. Spiritual change- As a result of PTG, one should have a more precise understanding of their spiritual life.

Interestingly, the authors found that women reported more benefits from traumatic experiences than men. However, the gap is small. Results show a deviation among participants—those who experienced *traumatic* events versus those who experienced *extraordinary* conditions. The researchers found that people who experienced traumatic events report more *positive changes and growth* as a result. There were some relationships found among people who experience PTG and certain personality traits like extroversion and optimism (Tedeschi & Calhoun, 1996).

Anne Marie Roepke is a clinical psychologist that describes PTG as a positive change in an individual's life. Dr. Roepke's research on the development of PTG and how psychological intervention can help people initiate the process and secure the benefits of this impacting personal growth. Roepke outlines areas of intervention that cultivates PTG. She explains what people think about the future is critical in finding meaning in life after a significant loss.

32

Chapter 10

Steps to Achieve Post-Traumatic Growth

WE KNOW THAT scene (and corresponding theme song) in the movie Rocky when Sylvester Stallone ran the steps. This scene has been replayed many times since 1976. Well, the steps that we will take towards achieving PTG will not look as triumphant as that (at least not at first). We will not be running up the stairs like Sylvester Stallone, full speed ahead, and then fist-pumping at the top by the museum entrance. The steps towards PTG are an endurance building type of training. The first part, and likely the hardest part, is that we must let ourselves *fall*. I mean, *fall flat on our face.*

When we hit the rapids hard, the natural desire is to fight the rush of the raging water; this is a mistake.

As our River Rat instructed us, "Don't fight the rapids, relax, and go with the flow."

When we experience trauma or stressful life events, we want to dance around the pain and hurt. We don't *let* ourselves entirely fall or allow our hearts to be broken and shattered in disappointment, fear, or any real, profound emotion. We want to dance around the pain and hurt by utilizing other tools:

- ☐ Denial

- ☐ Blame

- ☐ Mind/emotion-altering substances

- ☐ Unhealthy relationships

- ☐ Even things that appear to be healthy at face value, such as hobbies or projects

These tools are not necessarily harmful (not all of them), but the point is that we employ them as a means to *cope* with the pain and hurt by *avoiding the pain and hurt.*

36

Chapter 11

Begin the Process of Post-Traumatic Growth

TO BEGIN THE process of PTG, we must let go of the stronghold we have on these tools that help us avoid our emotions. *Let go and feel it* ("Don't fight the rapids, relax and go with the flow."). We might find that it's easier and less stressful to avoid shutting out those painful emotions. Keeping ourselves busy (avoiding feel) can prove after *much* time and effort, we might still find ourselves sad and empty. The proper tools we use to cope will come in handy later, but for now, we need to let ourselves feel the pain.

Step 1: Shattered into a Million Pieces

PTG begins with letting life hit where it hurts and accepting that it hurts. It hurts a lot! **Pay**

attention to this critical step because *this is where we will likely learn and see the most valuable information.* We will later build upon this once the pain and hurt have lifted a bit (i.e., the later steps towards PTG).

The Class V rapids have delivered us to a waterfall. Over the crest, we flow. We find ourselves freefalling down the waterfall, sinking quickly down to the bottom of the river.

We find ourselves under the waterfall wholly submerged in the water.

It's like we're sitting at the bottom of a black hole, after falling in headfirst. This submersion shakes us, resulting in fear and emotional dizziness as we try to wrap our head around the situation. We can't breathe. The feeling of death is very present. Panic takes over; we fight for survival with broken pieces of the wave-punching paddle raft splintered around us.

Suddenly we also realize we managed to survive the fall somehow. As our mind begins to process what has happened to us, we start to wish that we hadn't survived.

"Wouldn't *it have been better*?" we ask yourself (or *plead* to God). "*If I would have just DIED so that I wouldn't have to live this pain*!" This thought may pop into our mind time and time again throughout Step 1, and some will experience and entertain this thought more vividly and frequently than others.

Human beings have a natural propensity to avoid pain. Pain (whether physical or emotional) doesn't feel right, and we like to feel good. The desire to feel good is driven by and derived from the nucleus accumbens (Nac), primitive, the pleasure-seeking part of the human brain. Real or not, it is tied, paradoxically, to our motivation to survive. Pain is a clue that our life is fragile. So, we sometimes prefer *death* rather than having to experience pain because we want to avoid injury.

Pain represents a threat to our existence, plus we want to preserve our life. *Confusing, I know.*

Step 1 of PTG allows us to wallow in the rock bottom. People make the mistake of trying to expedite this step. It is unpleasant (see pain explanation above) and sometimes due to the well-intended but often erroneous advice from others who are watching us suffer and want to help. We might get advice urging us to "*think positive*" or "*try to move on*" as if those words will solve everything.

Advice from loved ones may even turn accusatory as the loved ones grow impatient with our suffering. Well, meaning people become aggravated with us because of the corresponding changes in our level of functioning. The trauma can sometimes strip us of our ability to live, work, and behave the way we once did well. Loved ones may mistakenly begin to attribute our behavior as *giving up* or *not trying hard enough*. We will start to internalize this and feel that it's our fault that we're just lying around, depressed, anxious, scared, a *dependent*. It's at this point when we will fell useless.

Notice that this <u>rejection from loved ones</u> (i.e., spouse, partner, family, friends) is also part of Step 1.

Step 1 will test us because we're at our *weakest*, fresh from the initial shock of our loss, and *another level* is added to the pain of loss. This additional pain is the *next level of* pain beyond any pain we have ever imagined. When we need our loved ones the most, some of them will become angry with us. Some of them will turn their backs, abandoning us when we need them the most.

Trauma and pain are intangibles: We can't see them or measure them to show the extent of the damage to someone else (or even to ourselves). We can see a tumor (on an MRI), measure cancer (through blood work); however, we can't provide any real, documented data of emotional damage. There's no X-Ray that the doctor can show our loved ones (and us) and say, "*Yep, there's where he hits rock bottom, right there" or "Right here, this little mass, that's her pain and suffering."*

Loved ones may expect us to move on faster than we're able; this will cause conflict or even the severance of some relationships. The good thing is that we will *know* who the loyal and genuine people in our life are because the kinships that last through Step 1 are the good ones.

What a fantastic thing when we can offer absolutely *nothing* to someone, but they still stick around. This discovery is the (probably the only) positive thing about Step 1 (at least at face value) because we can (finally) let go of superficial and toxic people. We may not see the value *during* Step 1 because we need (and want) all the help and support from others. Still, we will later learn that getting rid of the excess baggage of negative persons will give us some much-needed room to grow throughout our PTG journey of personal change.

Once we have allowed ourselves to process and feel the pain of our loss and step out of denial, our mind and body will gradually adjust to this new reality. Step 1 is a lot like getting ourselves through the most significant and most challenging adjustment in our life to something new. It just takes us a while to fully wrap our mind around this sudden, unexpected shift that happened faster than we can process.

Step 1 could be likened to when we get a new pair of good running shoes; they might feel tight and constricted when we initially wear them.

The first few walks, or jogs might be painful. We might even want to pull out our old ones from the donation bin because those were so *comfortable and familiar*. Although once we break them in, we feel like we're gliding effortlessly, and we run full speed ahead, grateful to give these new shoes a chance.

Step 2: Getting Up & Building on Our Positives

One of the most meaningful realizations that we will have about hitting rock bottom is that *"It can't get any worse than this."* Even if it *could* get any worse, we now feel we can survive *worse* because we've survived *this* loss. Therefore, we think that we can take *anything* that life throws our way. We know what it feels like to be scared, alone, depressed, and lost.

That dark path is no longer unknown. We know it like the palm of our hand. It's now very familiar because that darkness has been our constant companion for so long (too long). This awareness is relieving, though, because we realize that in a way, there is no more unpredictability. Unpredictability is the only thing that is probably more frightening than the trauma itself. We've gotten through the worst, then a *hint* of a hopeful thought will cross our mind, *"From here, the only way is up."*

Thankfully, with a life jacket, we are buoyant. The life jacket is a metaphor for the positive people, the ones whose help genuinely encourage. This support lifts us back up. Without these people, we would unmistakably drown at the bottom of the waterfall.

What do we do when the shock of loss leaves us less capable, less able, and less 'me'? We have only two choices. We can fight, or we can embrace it. Let me explain:

1) We can fight against this new reality.

This is the time when we try desperately to get our life back because we long for what we lost. Everything that made up our past before our life turned upside down.

Tring to gain back the loss would be like trying to swim back up the waterfall to reach the place we were before the troubled waters.

2) We can embrace this new life and this new 'me.'

We've spent a lot of time and energy trying to get our old life back, not realizing that the early life and that old 'me' no longer exist. Instead, we should embrace this new experience.

When we are trying to get back what we lost, we are losing our present. When we are looking back at what we lost, we are facing the wrong direction. To grow from our pain, we must look to our future.

Yes, we must turn around to face our future. In doing so, **we are turning our back on the past-on the loss**.

If we put our efforts into trying to get the past back, we will cycle through Steps 1 and 2 repeatedly. Repeating these steps means that we're not learning and not growing because the reality is, things will never be the same. *Nothing ever stays the same.*

If we embrace our new self and our new life, we will soon realize that it's a good thing that our life will never be the same again. Maybe there were aspects of our *"old life,"* our *pre-trauma life*, that weren't good for us. Conceivably some things needed to get washed away with the raging waters.

Amazingly enough, the churning water provides a cleansing. Imagine how a presser washer cleans. It cleans by leveraging pressurized water to a focused point, pushing away the grime.

Perhaps a washing machine would be a better explanation.

If our laundry had feelings, they would experience similar cries on each laundry day as we do during the trauma. Our clothes are placed into a situation whereby they are in the water, tossed about, sent spinning round and round, about 80 miles an hour, while beaten with paddles. Isn't that how we fell during the difficulty?

During Step 2, we will consider some of the critical functions, some of the *necessary* things that occurred as a result of the trauma. Unfortunately, we were either too stubborn, too comfortable, or too distracted to see this before.

This loss has an essential function in our life. During Step 2, we will start to feel a little better (physically and emotionally). When we begin feeling better, we should avoid using this energy to try to reach for the past in hopes of erasing the painful memories. Tring to remove the painful memories will lead to frustration and depression because we will swiftly realize that we can't get back the past. So, we must throw it out and ask ourselves, ***"What can I do now? How can I start anew*?"**

Depression is fueled by living in the past, and anxiety is driven by living in the future. Step 2 is about living and accepting the present. Step 2 is about acceptance, *considering* that our trauma is a gift in a perfect *disguise*. Trauma has stripped us of a plethora of things. At first, this felt like a punishment or a curse of some sort. However, when we lost everything we had, we have a renewed clarity to see ourselves. Many of us are seeing ourselves for the first time. When loss leaves us with what feels like *nothing*, we can learn our real strength. Think of it as a view of the soul.

These are our:

☐ Real qualities

☐ Abilities

☐ Uniqueness

☐ The things that no loss can take away because this is who you are

Those things that specify who we are don't disappear, no matter how horrible the trauma. They don't fade because those are the special and unique qualities about us.

Those are the qualities that we must *see* and fully acknowledge. Those are the positives that we will use and build upon to *get up and navigate our new journey*.

During Step 2, we may still go in and out of moments of fear and confusion. We realize that we aren't the same as we were before. We now know that we must figure somehow to move on with our life. We may find ourselves looking over the precipice and vividly seeing (or feeling) Step 1 again. We may feel like we're not strong enough yet, that we're not ready to move on; this is when we must ask ourselves, "*Who am I?*" At this stage, we have to remind ourselves of those qualities, that uniqueness about ourselves.

Think about the positives, the things that the loss didn't take. What are we able to do because of those positives? These special qualities that are unique to 'me' will help us understand our true identity. **Who are you**? We're more than what we're not able to do. What we're not able to do does not define us. Consider this during those moments of despair and confusion. Forget about what we *can't* do. We must tell ourselves, "*You will gain strength from what you can do.*" We need to take small steps towards anything that we can do right now. Small steps and small tasks are better than trying to tackle anything meaningful. Gradual, small, and successive steps are essential. Although we may not realize it yet, those small, steady steps are guiding us in the right direction.

Step 3: From Broken to Better (Phoenix from the ashes)

It's imperative to build on the positive. Building on the positives creates momentum. The journey feels less uphill, steadier, and less rocky. But that ever-present memory of the battle that brought us to this point provides an indescribable sense of gratitude. This battle also gives an increased ability to relish in all the gifts of the present.

The three steps of PTG are not meant to delineate this life-altering experience in an overly simplified box of an *"a, b, c; 1, 2, 3"* process. The steps describe the process and the distinct stages of this growth and rebirth that individuals experience after the trauma. Step 3 is not the pinnacle by any means. In Step 3, we're in the adolescents' stage of our journey and this new life we have been given and have paved for ourselves.

There is no way toward this gently, but when we went through that sudden, unexpected, rock bottom experience of loss, we *died*. In other words, we experienced a death—*Our death*. PTG is the process of starting anew through a vital failure. The damage is not only of things, people, goals, or money (even though we likely lost one or all those things too). It is the loss of our identity and the journey towards finding our '*self*' again.

Picture it this way; when we reached the bottom of the river (bottom of the waterfall), we died to our old way of life. As we burst forth from this watery grave, we are born into a new life-a fresh perspective on life.

The only difference between this type of death and the *other* type of death (i.e., the transformation of the *physical* body) is that we get to experience and watch our end in *real-time. This death* often occurs in an emotionally (and even physically) tortuous manner. Death can occur in many ways and not necessarily at the "*end*" of our life when our body gives out when we experience loss and the accompanying drastic life changes. In a sense, we experience a fore of death because the experience makes us start all over again.

54

Chapter 12

Another Way to Look at Things

ANOTHER WAY TO look at a loss is the things we acquired before; a lot of what (or sometimes everything that) worked, lived for or strived for disappears. We are, in a sense, left as infants, having to re-learn and re-experience life again. In Step 1, we are restored and have to (literally) learn to get back on our feet and take one step at a time to try to move forward again. We are helpless in a sense, practically (or literally) dependent on others to survive. In Step 2, we are a child, trying to learn and absorb our new environment, and even regressing to infancy at times, when things get overwhelming and scary. In Step 3, we are an adolescent, ready to embark on our path in life, but still gaining knowledge, experience, and insight. Someday soon, we can use our positives to do something great.

Step 3 involves connecting the dots of your PTG. Things start to make sense. Why everything happened makes sense. Our understanding of gratitude grows, as we're thankful for not only the present but also for those problematic experiences that led us to the present. Our traumatic event took everything from us. We can see who we are, without the distractions of our previous life. Now we can use our positives to build a new, more genuine, and more meaningful life.

We're designed to be more than a survivor—we-re intended to thrive. Our loss is to for us to experience growth, development, and insight. We may begin to realize that our PTG has also kindled something deeper within.

We must consider that there is yet another purpose to all the difficulty and pain that we went through that maybe it's *not all about 'me.' We will* find whether we can use our experience to help and inspire others who are going through dark times. We begin to understand that PTG is not just a *self-*oriented experience. PTG changes each of us so that we can use our positives that we now see and understand better than ever. We should *give back* and make some positive contribution that will impact those around us. We can use our difficulty to *add value* to someone else. That is the ultimate growth-to be able to turn a seemingly negative situation into personal growth and to let our struggle guide others in need.

Conclusion

NOW IT MAKES sense. Had we not gone through those difficult times, we might have never stopped long enough to consider how we can live a life of true meaning and purpose. We often get on this fast track in our lives. We think mostly of goal achievement, professional and economic growth, and primarily acquiring as many *things* as we can. No wonder life sometimes felt *so empty*. Maybe we subconsciously knew that our lives lacked meaning, and we secretly wished to exchange for something better.

Trauma and life-changing events stop us in our tracks so that we can remake our life journey because the path that we were on was surely not taking us towards any semblance of happiness or wholeness. PTG makes us truly understand the value of reassessing our life priorities. It helps us to consider how we can somehow make a meaningful contribution to others and the community around us. PTG helps us recognize *what matters, what is essential, what is the principal purpose-personal growth and helping others.*

References

Hefferon, K., Grealy, M., & Mutrie, N. (2009). Post-Traumatic profile-threateningeatening physical illness: A systematic review of the qualitative literature. *British Journal of Health Psychology*, 14, 343-378.

Mangelsdorf, J. & Ed, M. (2015). What makes a thriver? Unifying the concept of Post-Traumatic and postecstatic grow. *Frontiers in Psychology*, 6, 1-17.

Post-Traumatic Growth in the aftermath of trauma: A literature review about related factors and application contexts. *Psychology, Community & Health*, 2(1), 43-54.

Rocky (1976): https://m.imdb.com/title/tt0075148/

Roepke, A. M. (2013). Gains without pains? Grow after positive events. *The Journal of Positive Psychology*, 8(4), 280-291.

Roepke, A. M. (n.p.). Research. Retrieved from https://www.annemarieroepke.com

Sheikh, A. (2008). Post-Traumatic Growth in trauma survivors: Implications for practice. *Counseling Psychology Quarterly*, 21(1), 85-97.

Tedeschi, R. G. & Calhoun, L. G. (1996). The Post-Traumatic Growth Inventory: measuring the positive legacy of trauma. *Journal of Traumatic Stress*, 9 (3), 455-471.

NOC Ocoee River. https://noc.com/plan-your-trip/ocoee-river

About the Author

TIMOTHY CARTER WAS born in North Georgia, USA, to loving parents. He is the second of three children raised in this pastoral home. He has served as Pastor, Assistant Pastor, Counselor, Prison Chaplin, Ministerial Care Director, President of the Ministerial Association, Professional Speaker, and Storyteller.

He is the author of several books, blogs, newspapers, and international journal articles.

Carter holds degrees of Bachelor of Science in Pastoral Ministries, with a concentration in Counseling from Lee University (2005); Master of Divinities with a concentration in Counseling from Pentecostal Theological Seminary (2008).

Carter is a Bishop with Church of God, Cleveland, TN.; License Community Service

Chaplain; Licensed Level 4 Church Consultant; Christian Counselor.

64

Other Books by

Timothy R. Carter

Classical Explanation of Salvation

Credit Repair: Your Comprehensive Guide

Ditch the Junk: How to Have a Successful Yard Sale

Vision: See it Achieve It

Connect with

Timothy R. Carter

Website: timothyrcarter.com

Facebook: https://www.facebook.com/Timothy-Carter-Author-499971137072277/?ref=settings

Twitter: @TimothCarterPhD

Amazon: amazon.com/author/timothycarterphd